Writings From The Heart

Nupur Upadhyaya

BookLeaf Publishing

Presentation by *BookLeaf Publishing*

Web: www.bookleafpub.com

E-mail: info@bookleafpub.com

ISBN: 9789357747899

First edition 2024

DEDICATION

To my dear mother, who inspires me to be the best version of myself on any given day. You're my best friend, my guiding light, and the reason I function as a human being.

To my dear father, who is the kindest, most caring, and has taught me self-reliance. I never express it out loud but I love you and that will never change.

To my cute brother, you will forever be the younger one, please get used to it, and do not, for the love of all, copy my bad habits. Love you lots!

To all of my friends who stuck with me through thick and thin, who lent me an ear for countless rambles, who inspired me by just being themselves, this is a heartfelt thank-you to you as well.

Lastly, a huge round of applause to the teachers who had the patience to teach me proper grammar because I know now how hard it was, you have my eternal gratitude. (Yes, this includes you mother!)

Smile Again

Her Heart full of mercy
Her soul so pure
Her thoughts so deep
She has every cure

Her beautiful smile
That twinkle in her eyes
The touch of her hands
Takes me to fairyland

When she gave birth to me
Showering love affectionately
She devoted all her life
To care for and raise her child

With her melodious voice
A song of her choice
She sang a lovely tune
And along danced the moon

Her words were sweet as honey
At the time I didn't understand
For I was still so little
Trying to clap with both my hands

Tears streamed down her face
And a big smile that conveyed
Her ecstasy when I laughed out
Hearing her song and clapped loud

The golden moments passed too fast
She wished sometimes to relive them, Alas!
It is a time long gone they say
It cannot be turned back again

If perchance I could, I certainly would
Try my best to traverse in time
I'd bring back all those precious memories
To make my mother smile again

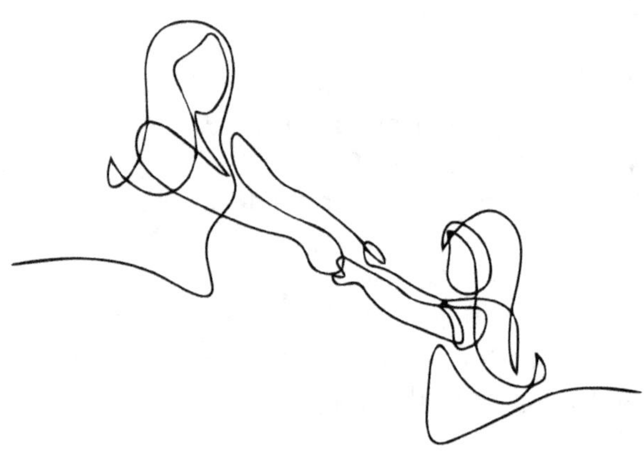

Like a Butterfly

As she breaks through her shell
And spreads out her wings
With that sparkle in her eyes
And her lovely, beautiful wings

She stops for a moment
And stars for her destination
She stumbles, and she falls
She is losing her patience

She stands up on her feet
And tries it once again
She's determined to reach her goal
She knows it's not in vain

Her efforts soon grow stronger
She fights her way back
Her faith is what she holds onto
She's picking up pace too fast

Her prolonged struggle makes her weak
She hides her tears till she weeps
And others look down upon her
Beaming at her bruised knees

But she doesn't give up so soon
She is determined to reach the moon
She gets up and follows the way
That leads her to that perfect place

Where she's received with dignity
And is treated equally
While those who try to take her down
Receive a reply that makes them frown

Thinking thus, she starts afresh
Armed with a new zeal and breadth
And now the little butterfly
Has spread out her wings to fly
And off she goes towards the sky
Free from bounds to live her life

Yearly Wisdom

The first month of the year when I fell sick
thrice
It taught me how to take care of my
half-immunity life

The second brought gusts of cold winds
throughout
Making me realize the importance of
warmth inside out

Third beaconed me to work hard and have
fun alongside
Alas! My laziness overtook me, ruining my
plans alike

Fourth was when I should've studied and
prepped in class
Guess it taught me not to delay till the last

Fifth started with pressurized exams and
long nights
Made me ruminate how fast time flies

The sixth was scorching hot, livid with
flames

Reminiscent of global warming, that
desperately needs to be chained

Seventh was humid with no rain in sight
Shouldn't have wasted water during baths
in winter time

Number eight resumed the classes when I
met friends after a while
In their absence life would not be
worthwhile

Ninth was all about stability and normality
While tenth pleasant with festivals of
joviality

Eleventh was all studies and getting serious
for exams
More like daytime sleeping for late-night
crams

Twelfth began quite crisp and cheery
Time for Christmas and holiday-making
merry

All the different seasons had a story of
their own
Sowing and reaping them like a seed till I'm
grown

And when the clock ticks twelve on the last
day the last night
I'll be a different person with a whole new
chapter to write

New lessons to be learned, new people to
be met,
New promises to keep, new limits to test

A little cup of those memories gathered in
a nest,
Preserved and protected even when life
comes to a rest

Thank You

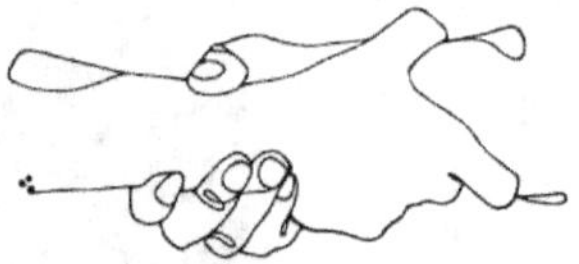

When my world was lonely
With no hope of any sunshine
You opened the doors
That led to my heart

When I sat alone at nights
And no one cared to come around
You showed up as a friend
Who gave me a hand

You showed me what life is
When you spread smiles around
You made me feel special
And not to back down

The darkness seemed to fade away
With rays of hope so bright
All the colours sprinkled over
My life just seemed so right

The oceans scream, the mighty waves
The clouds themselves paved the way
The winds, they played a soulful tune
While my sorrows drift away and away

The world is ours with you around
Together, you and I, we can make it through
A true friend I have made today
So here is a little Thank-you!

Adolescent Dreams

Just like the shining stars
In the night glimmering bright
I hope in my heart
That you would come by

Listening to your song
Like a whisper in the wind
I get lost in a trance
Of your sweet lullaby

Sometimes I sit and wonder
Are you a dream? A fantasy?
Too far from my reach
Yet so close to me

I had my walls up
Until you found me
But it's not so easy
To have faith and belief

Yet, I don't know how
And I don't know why
I don't hide from you
I trust you completely

Never met you for real
But there's a voice inside
Saying you're not just a friend
I'm falling for you slowly

Should I stop myself here?
And preserve our friendship
Or should I let you know
All my desires and feelings!

First Crush

What will you think?
If I say I miss you!
What will you say?
If I say I adore you!

Will you even smile?
When I compliment you!
Or will you be sad?
Because of my naivety!

What will you think?
If I idolize you!
What will you say?
If I try to flatter you!

Will you be a little happy?
When I appreciate you!
Or will you be a little sad?
Because of my naivety!

What will you think?
When I tell you about my dreams!
What will you say?
When do I tell you they're about you?

Will you be elated?
If I treasure your presence!
Or will you be sorrowful?
Because of my naivety!

What will you think?
When I say I like you!
What will you say?
When I do tell you my feelings?

Will you be ecstatic?
If my sentiments are true!
Or will you be angry?
Because of my naivety!

What will you think?
When I relish your touch!
What will you say?
When I'm infatuated with you!

Will you be delighted?
When you meet me in person!
Or will you be disgusted?
Because of my naivety!

What will you think?
When I'm not what you'd hoped to see!
What will you say?
When I'm not what you thought I'd be!

Will you be content?
When I'm not as good as you portrayed me!
Or will you be unwilling?
Because of my naivety!

What will it be then?
When I say that I fell for you!

Will you be ignorant?
Or will you agree willingly?

Will you be miserable?
Or will you be at peace?

Will you loathe my very presence?
Or will you befriend me?

Will you harbour hate and rage?
Or will you be carefree?

What will you say if I mean every word I asked?

What will you think if I meant everything I
thought?

What will you do if I fancy you too much in my
dreams?
Will it be the same if I tell you all my feelings?

What will you say if I wish to have you for my
own?
What will you think if I feel something I cannot
control?

What will you do if I fantasize too much?
Will I forever be naive and not deserve such
love?

Or will I ever find someone whom I actually
deserve?

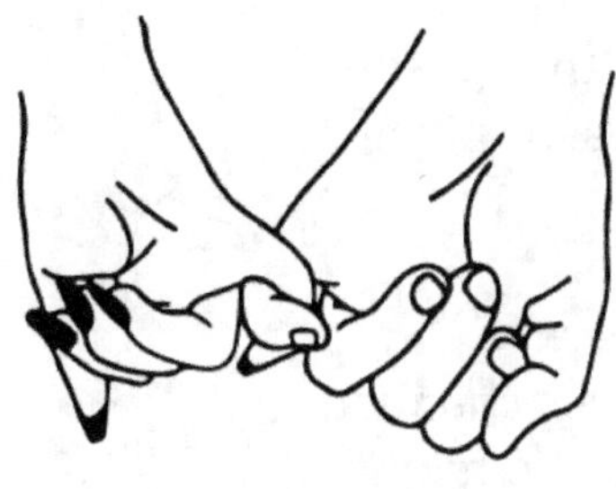

Reminiscence

I made a friend
I didn't know much about
Who had his walls up
All the while

Never had I seen
Someone so closed
He was a bit different
Yet so uptight

A weird one
I thought he was
Who lived his life
The way he liked

Try as I may
To open those doors
That held the reason
To his present plight

All my efforts
Wasted in vain
For he never changed
Even when he might

He had a dark secret
Or maybe just sorrow

Something in his past
Which he'd always deny

Neither sweet talk
Nor admonishment
Could change his views
Or affect his mind

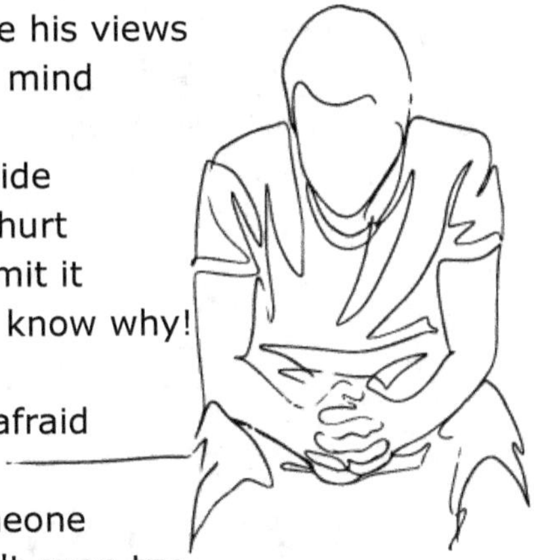

But deep inside
I know he's hurt
He won't admit it
I don't even know why!

Maybe he's afraid
Just like me
To trust someone
So he doesn't even try

Or maybe it's me
Who's afraid of the fall
Yet I don't give up
Even as time goes by

His voice is so pure
A little soft and smooth
Something that I love
Which I can't deny

Although fun to talk to
He hides from all
Has music in his head
A bit of a crazy guy

Hoping in my heart
That he might still remember
Me or just some memories
If we ever say goodbye

Mathematical Valentine

Cupid's birthday around the corner
Fourteenth was excited
A dimensionless hall of pink and red
Splotched with flowers white

Seven roses a week before
Bent down on a knee of nine chocolates
A 10-dollar teddy with 11 promises to keep
Proposed to eight on a Saturday

Two days before the bash
A lone hug found its keeper the next day
Sealing the promises with a simple kiss
Reminiscing about the sunset days

And so they all went, hand in hand
Tying their knots with every mortal
A year they had, to revisit them all
So bid Adieu on Valentine's Day formal!

Virtual Friend

Sometimes I wish
I had someone like you
You seem a distant dream,
One that I can't acclaim
Maybe if I deserve I'll do!
But as I don't,
I wait! I'll Wait,
For someone
Someone like you.

Distance is much,
Yet feels so surreal
Talking to you
Never met you for real
But feels so close,
Feels so true!

Have I lost my mind?
Is it just a dream?
Pinch me, wake me now!
I'm lost in thoughts
It is self-consuming
I don't even know how!

Miss you when I'm lonely
When I'm shattered from inside
Hoping to meet you somehow
Feel so lucky sometimes
Such a humble person
I've come to know about

Wish that maybe someday,
I'll finally meet you in real
All my thoughts all my dreams,
Will cease to be unreal
Hoping and praying that,
You won't turn your back on me.

Maybe I'm not what you expect.
Maybe I'm not smart enough.
Maybe I'm a pessimist about myself.
I know you'll change that fact,
Unless all that I see is,
Just a sweet fantasy of you.

Fearing you will not be happy,
To meet me when you finally do
Fearing that what I knew was just,
A Fairy tale, nothing true
Fearing that my presence might,
Might be, a disgust to you.

My hopes will be pushed aside,
All my dreams crushed alike
To escape it I'll forever hide,
Unless you be the shinning knight,
And rescue me from this plight.

I'll be glad of what I have
Since I know you I've always been
Forever will I cherish this bond
With you as my friend, every day,
A new chapter will begin!

Laments of Royalty (The Dreaming Princess)

Once upon a time
A princess in distress
Wanted to live her life
As her own mistress

But her parents
Wouldn't let her out
They wanted her secured
Day and night throughout

Guess she was just too naive
To listen to their talk
Took a chance at liberty
Without knowing where to walk

She had always been too bubbly
Had always done the wrong
Even got too many scoldings
But never corrected that wrong

Soon she fell into the trap
She was to stay away from
Being wrong as she'd always been
Did the unthinkable and was gone

She hid away all her secrets
About the one that could be a prince
Who wasn't what she'd ever want
But she wouldn't listen

Being the princess as she claimed
She took to blaming the rest
Lies after lies she said
But didn't try to face the test

But somewhere in her mind
She had the nagging doubt
That once caught she'd lose everything
Even the love and trust somehow

Being naive as she was
She didn't spare it any glance
And that is just how she ruined
Her possibility of a second chance

Meeting with the Romeo
Every now and then
She soon got discovered
By her best friend

Even she was skeptical
About who the prince was
Tried to talk her out of it
But failed no matter what

One day as it came upon chance
The princess started to think
What would it have been like
If she could change everything

Had she not been so persistent
Then maybe she would have been smart
Had she not been in such a rush
Her life wouldn't be so hard

"What have I done to myself?"
"I'm so lost inside!"
"Why did I not think about it?"
"Why couldn't I decide what's right!"

That all this trouble
And all the precious time
Is not worth this person
But one that fate decides

Alas! She was too late
For soon her secret was found
That was when she lost her faith
And since then, she can't stand her ground

Never been trusted ever since
All her life she'll never be
No matter the circumstances
Never again she'll ever be free
She deserves it though

Deserves all sorrow
All the pain she put her family through
That Fate has borrowed

Now she's done
Fighting her own demons
She can't control her thoughts
Can't push aside those demons

Haunted by nightmares
Of worthlessness and futility
She tries to fulfill her desires
Dreaming about serenity

But dreams are dreams
Not harsh reality
Which she has to endure
Using tools of morality

If not then else!
She'll be abandoned for life
Without a family without a home
She'll be left alone to thrive

Aware of the horrific outcomes
Of a mistake made a second time
She doesn't want to give up so soon
Neither wants the hope to die
Wishing to be the perfect girl
That every prince would always like

She dreams away about the one
Who would love her just as she might

But life isn't a fairy tale
It's only of the harsh kind
Her dreams are made of all those wishes
That fate has completely declined

But once again
She forgot herself
Got lost in thoughts
Of someone else

And now she has to pay the price
And she knows she can't win anytime
Because if she tries to cross the line
She knows she'll lose herself this time!

Her

She has the patience
She has the light
She has everything the world has always
denied

She has the courage
She has the power
She has the goodness the world has kept
afar

She has the beauty
She has the soul
She has the sweetest voice that can control

She has the sorrow
She has the pain
She has the time to heal the wounds she
gained

She has the freedom
She has the sight
She has the blessings the world has pushed
aside

She has the virtue
She has the mind
She has the wisdom the world can never
find

She has the glory
She has the grace
She has the smiles that once were off her
face

She has the story
She has the love
She has the greatest gifts from up above

She has the journey
She has the life
She has everything the world can't satisfy

She has the spirit
She has the key
She is everything the world can never see

She is the daughter whose parents you'd
feel proud to be

She is the sister who'll turn your sorrow
into glee
She is the mother whose love is always free

She is the woman every girl aspires to be

Created by the Almighty

Disguised as a blessed dream

She is mankind's greatest being

She is a woman

(Dedicated to all the women out there -
Remember, You Matter)

Because you can

You can be weak
You can be strong
You can face your fears if you want

No one can force you
To copy the rest
You can prove your worth to them even
through a test

You can be wrong
You can be right
You can shine like the stars of the night

No one can make you
To follow them behind
You can be the one leading them in line

You can be harsh
You can be soft
You can be all that you think you're not

No one can control you
To bind you in those chains
You can break them easily for the world to see
- You Remain

Human

I might be blind
But I can still hear

I might be dumb
But I can still feel

My nose might not work
But I can still eat

My legs might give out one day
But I can still knead

I may not be the breadwinner
Or the top artist
Or that government agent who has
everything

But, I'm still human
I can feel, I can hear, I can taste and I will
not kneel

My colour doesn't define me
My lineage is nothing different
But I'm still special, I'm still me!

I can work all night or sleep in the
meetings
I can cry without a voice and laugh
without it too
I can be the brightest or wallow in my
misery
I can shine like a bird in the wind or be a
shallow queen

I have the freedom to cherish and bonds
to make
People to meet, and meet them I will
someday

Within my heart are emotions I cannot
describe
And a coldness that makes me numb, a
fear that makes me cry

A human through and through
Doesn't matter the religion or the race
I make mistakes,
And I plan to make more someday

Because that's how I'll learn to stand on
my own rights
My feet might be weak, but I'll still make
it out alright
I've dreamt of dreams and drowned in
sorrows

I've learned to live life today and
tomorrow

So go ahead, your verdict matters little
Your judgment is skewered and your
thought process nil
I'm happy today, content with what I have
I'm a miracle to those who care, it is my
story that my memories will gather

This,
Is me!

Little Dream

The little broken pencil
Was all that I owned
The little piece of cloth
Was all that I had worn
The little roof of leaves
Was all I could manage
Without the light for my eyes to see

The little rugged paper
Was all that I found
The little scrap of meal
Was all that I ate
The little drops of water
Were all that I drank
Amidst the dark where my eyes couldn't see

The little burning lamp
Was all that I had
The little rats or mice
Were my only company
The little squeaky sound
Was all I could hear
In the dark silence surrounding me

The little friend that I had
Was all I wanted back
The little ray of hope
Was what I had preserved
The little dream of mine
Was all that I desired
To return the light for my eyes to see

The Journey of time

Time ticks by
Have I lost it all?
Have I given up way too fast?
All the dreams that I had
All the good or the bad
Have I lost them to the past?

Time ticks by
It waits for none!
Not a victim of this world
Not a mortal being
It follows everything
But it flies by like a bird.

Time ticks by
When it's lost for once
It's never coming back to stay
Chase all your precious dreams
'Cause time is like a stream
That'll drown them if you're late.

Time ticks by
Is it not aware?
Of the struggles that it puts us through!
All the troubles that we face
No matter the colour or the race
It's just the same for me and you.

Words

There's a story written in every word
Every breath of sunlight
In the taste of air and flight of colours on
sinewy wings
The feel of evening light cascading along and
the sweet lullaby of morning dew

There's a story to be heard in every word
That was, is, will be a song
Of silent vows and desperate nights with
dreams infinite
A melody of the rhyme of life or lives
Beautiful, sinful, dangerous, fragile
Human enough yet inhuman alike

A story of a word is magically alight
With pleasure and pains and memories and
twittering
Of wonder, of will or woes and vice
Of wise yet suffering, mute and blind
Of feelings and emotions of day and night

It's a story of nothing and anything and
everything all at once
Be it the heart's desires or the world's demise

Music

I have a soul
A life to behold
Pure yet bold
A story untold

Conjuring tricks
With stylized remix
A Careful Practice
Or Spontaneous fix

A rhythm in the street
A melody incomplete
A frivolous treat
Synced to your heartbeat

Born of spurious reality
With a hint of obscure clarity
Scented with seasonal sensuality
Drinking from the glass of immortality

Peace

The land was painted forth
Flooded with mud and blood
The stench of the dead
Reeking through the air

The water smelled of fear
The forest residing doom
Silent screams of lost souls
Breaking through the sky

A lone figure stood, barely
Another rumble sounded far
The ground shuddered aloud
Agonizing wails intensified

Somewhere there.. A wolf howled
A messenger of the massacre
A shot was heard, seen, felt
The figure tumbled down, dead

Fire broke through and through
Burning red, the flooded draught
Marching forward on hopeless winds
Carrying away the ashes left behind

It didn't end as soon as it started
The scars, the burns, they never healed
The misery that started inside
Diminished the flicker of hope for the living
corpses

Black! Black, it screamed!
The picturesque scene following them
And when all began to rot in hell
Looking down upon the deathly stillness
They finally found it
And they called it .. Peace.

Déjà vu

An autumn winter
Bright yet cold
Walking along the brink
I saw him standing there
Heard him whisper
To the gusty wind
In a sing-song voice
Sharing secrets of the rain

He talked with eyes
With words of morning dew
His eyes, the colour of the Ocean
Crystal, like diamonds glistening

His voice a soft murmur
Deep and gently alluring to hear
His mere presence divine
A pleasure unlike any other, running wild

I was smitten I was scared
For I never felt something so pure
Extraordinary? It was magical to me
Like the world moved to reside in him

The rest was blurry
Like a haze gliding over
And just like that it ended
He was gone with the wind!

Baffled I was
Retracing my steps
I reached the fork in the woods
Paths plummeting to unknown depths
I took one
Oblivious of my destination
Maybe I woke up too soon
It was all blurry again

It all came crashing down
A weight settling on my shoulders
The yearning to find him was strong
An emotion foreign to me
Shattered and broken
Two words to surmise it all
And just like that, he came
Sealing away the torment within my walls

I couldn't help it this time
I screamed and flailed in vain
Fear choking me, pale white face
But then he whispered my name

Hope ignited, a spark, his touch
I felt it in my heart, I knew
He'd be with me always, I knew
A lone tear rolled down my cheek

And then they flooded back, the memories
Buried inside all this time, awakened
And I sobbed, I had found
The string that roped around me, protecting
me

It was him all along, every day
Consigned in the graveyard, all these years
I forgot how hard it was to lose him
I cried it away, the hurt and pain

But now I know he never left me
Now I know, I know he's in me
He was my rock, always has been
It's time to be with him, to be free

For the last time that day, she tore apart
The last time when she cried to sleep
When the rain stopped, she opened her eyes
At last, her corse had a peaceful dream.

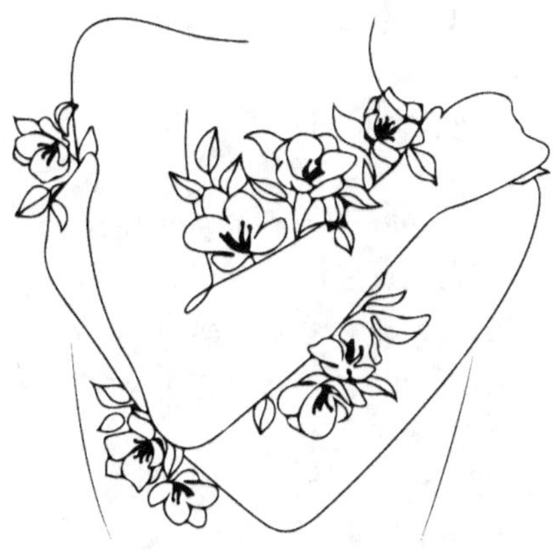

Life Cycle of Generations

An observer was he
Always far, yet nearer every day
Development, they named him
A new generation, a new way

She never knew what hatred was
She was always forgiving, kind
Mother Nature they called her
A beauty pure, sublime

He fell in love, hard and fast
She obliged, unwilling so
He was Satan, a warpath, demise
She couldn't escape his hold

Ebbing away, step by step
Her cries fell on deaf ears
His creators ruthless as him
Fuelled his growth with her tears

"They don't mean it", he said
She made a mistake - 'believed'
Slowly tearing her apart, he relished
When her shallow breath bereaved

And then it all dawned upon
His creators faced a different wrath
Destruction followed, shadowed around
Indescribable its path

He was numb, she was dying
Remorse, regret, restlessness, resign
It was all felt by meagre survivors
And fragments that were left behind

'Anger' the war raged - creators against creation
She was the witness destined to survive
And when all was gone, all was still
She wailed at the loss, yet blissfully alive

When the world awakened at the last call
The cycle restarted, revived, amplified
Harmony accomplished, broken bonds tied
Balance restored while nature thrived

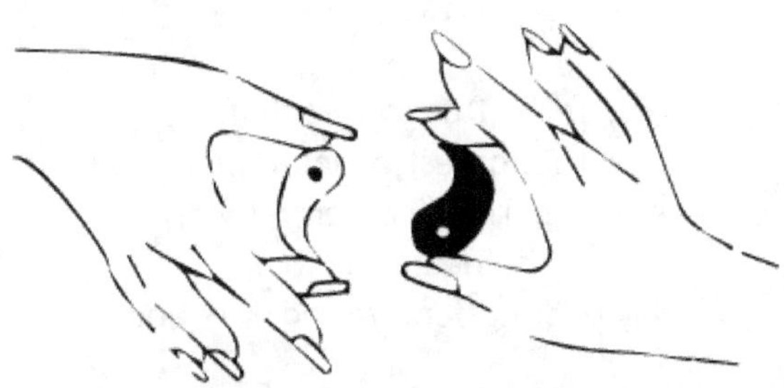

The Way Uphill

Bare rooted the trees,
Standing tall in the scorching heat
Barren lands, the arid outcasts
Deprived, driven with a speck of green peeking
out from somewhere under

Fall leaves scattered hither thither
Like a canvas of dead trodden leaves
Waiting to be blown away with nature's winds
Just to pollute the so-called developed lands of
the day

Far far yet nearer each minute
The majestic mountains
Greener yet barren, colder yet warmer than
the hearts of some
My destination, yet not the end

For then comes the horizon I'm yet to
accomplish
Snake-like winding tracks leading up the
steep-sloped trail
Of the temple sheltered in these high woods

Once existent but now dried as a bone, the
waterfalls, the riverbed
From which arise the rocky boulders blocking
the pathway
Still from the lifeless stones peek
The twigs of green, a reminder that life goes on

This little adventure might halt,
Yet the great journey will persist
Even after reaching the zenith